GIANT OCEAN ANIMALS

GIANT SQUID

Deep-Sea Creature

BY EMMANUEL MARSHALL

Enslow PUBLISHING

Please visit our website, www.enslow.com. For a free color catalog of all our high-quality books, call toll free 1-800-398-2504 or fax 1-877-980-4454.

Cataloging-in-Publication Data
Names: Marshall, Emmanuel.
Title: Giant squid / Emmanuel Marshall.
Description: Buffalo, NY : Enslow Publishing, 2027. | Series: Giant ocean animals | Includes glossary and index.
Identifiers: ISBN 9781978550629 (pbk.) | ISBN 9781978550636 (library bound) | ISBN 9781978550643 (ebook)
Subjects: LCSH: Giant squids--Juvenile literature. | Squids--Juvenile literature.
Classification: LCC QL430.3.A73 M377 2027 | DDC 594.58--dc23

Published in 2027 by
Enslow Publishing
2544 Clinton Street
Buffalo, NY 14224

Portions of this work were originally authored by Angela Lim and published as *Giant Squid*. All new material in this edition was authored by Emmanuel Marshall.

Cover Designer: Joshua Olson
Interior Designer: Joshua Olson
Editor: Noah Riccardi

Photo Credits: Cover, p. 1 Random Rolls/Shutterstock.com; pp. 4–5 R. Catanach/NOAA; pp. 6, 26–27, 29 Stefan Claesson/NOAA; pp. 6–7 Kunhui Chih/iStockphoto; pp. 8–9 Islandjems-Jemma Craig/Shutterstock.com; pp. 10–11 Tammy616/iStockphoto; pp. 12–13 Benoit B./iStockphoto; pp. 14–15, 22–23 NOAA; pp. 16–17 ArliftAtoz2205/Shutterstock.com; p. 18 Dental Education/Shutterstock.com; p. 19 Boome/Shutterstock.com; pp. 20–21 skyblue16/iStockphoto; pp. 24–25 wildest animal/Shutterstock.com.

Printed in China

CPSIA compliance information: Batch #QS27ENS: For further information contact Enslow Publishing, at 1-800-398-2504.

TABLE OF CONTENTS

CHAPTER 1

MYSTERIOUS GIANTS 5

CHAPTER 2

DARK WATERS 11

CHAPTER 3

BODY PARTS 17

CHAPTER 4

PREY AND PREDATORS 23

Test Your Knowledge · 28

Glossary · 30

For More Information · 31

Index · 32

ALVIN

CHAPTER 1

MYSTERIOUS GIANTS

Giant squid are large creatures that live in the deep ocean. Little is known about these mysterious animals. Very few images exist of living giant squid.

Scientists try to take pictures of giant squid by sending robots with cameras deep underwater.

Giant squid live up to their name. The largest one ever seen was 43 feet (13 m) long. It may have weighed up to 2,000 pounds (907 kg).

A giant squid's eight arms are all different lengths.

Giant squid live in almost complete darkness.

Giant squid have eight arms and two tentacles.

COLOSSAL COUSINS

Giant squid are related to another species called colossal squid. Even less is known about colossal squid. They may be even larger than giant squid.

Nautiluses are cephalopods. They can have more than 90 tentacles.

Giant squid are **cephalopods**. This group of animals includes squid, octopuses, and similar creatures. They all have soft bodies, arms, and tentacles.

336°

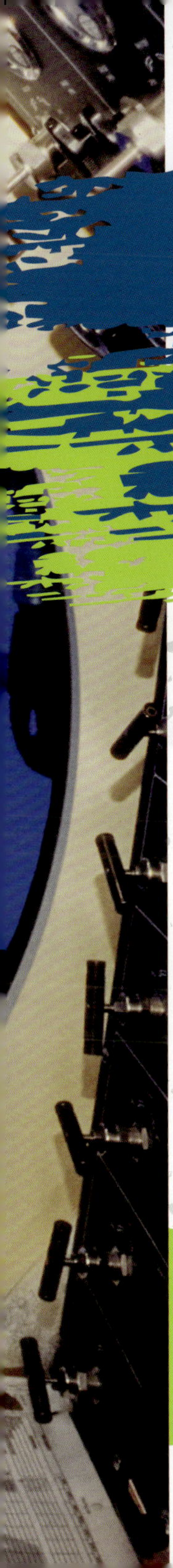

CHAPTER 2

DARK WATERS

Giant squid live in oceans all around the world. But they are less common in **tropical** and **polar** waters. They can survive at depths of 3,280 feet (1,000 m).

Scientists use submarines to explore the deep ocean where giant squid live.

Fishers shared stories about giant monsters that attacked ships.

This very deep water is hard to explore. Scientists got the first video of a live giant squid in 2006.

People have explored less than 20 percent of the ocean.

MONSTERS OF THE DEEP

Fishers told tales about the kraken. It was a monster with tentacles that could sink ships. These stories could be based on the giant squid.

Before 2006, scientists could only study carcasses. Bodies of giant squid sometimes wash up on shore. They can get tangled in fishing nets.

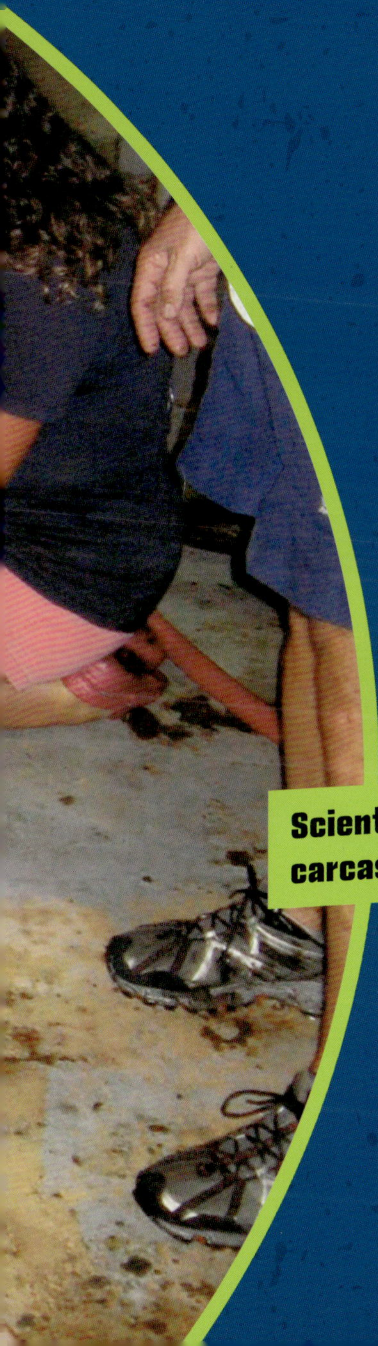

Scientists study the carcass of a giant squid.

ale meets Squid for lunch

CHAPTER 3

BODY PARTS

A giant squid's body is called a mantle. Its arms and tentacles are covered in suction cups. The suction cups have sharp edges. They grab **prey** and stop it from escaping.

A museum in Australia displays a giant squid's body in a tank.

To move, a squid sucks water into its mantle. Then it pushes the water back out. This moves the squid forward.

Suction cups help squid grab and hold onto food.

A squid's mantle is often shaped like a bell.

A giant squid has three hearts.

A squid's beak is parrotlike.

A giant squid has a sharp **beak**. The beak slices fish into small pieces. The squid's tongue is covered with rows of teeth.

CHEW YOUR FOOD!

A giant squid's brain is shaped like a donut. Food passes through the center hole. Food that is too large can damage the squid's brain.

CHAPTER 4

PREY AND PREDATORS

Giant squid eat shrimp and fish. They grip prey with two feeding tentacles. They use their arms to pull prey toward their mouths.

A giant squid's two feeding tentacles are extra long.

Few animals attack giant squid. The sperm whale is the squid's main **predator**.

Sperm whales are known for their huge heads.

Giant squid steal food from one another.

A giant squid's eyes can be larger than basketballs.

People have studied giant squid for hundreds of years.

The large eyes of giant squid help them see sperm whales from far away. Squid can escape by squirting dark ink.

ACTIVE HUNTERS

Many large sea creatures move slowly. For this reason, they only eat dead animals. But giant squid are quick. They are able to attack live prey.

TEST YOUR KNOWLEDGE

Take this quiz to test your knowledge.

1. Write a sentence describing what a giant squid's body looks like.

2. Do you think giant squid are dangerous? Why or why not?

3. How do giant squid move through the ocean?

- **A.** They use their arms and tentacles to swim.
- **B.** They spin their suction cups.
- **C.** They push water out of their mantles.

4. Why is it difficult to find giant squid?

- **A.** They are only found in tropical waters.
- **B.** Much of where they live is still unexplored.
- **C.** They blend in with the water.

5. What does **mysterious** mean in this book?

*Little is known about these **mysterious** animals.*

A. something people are interested in
B. something that is well-known
C. something people don't know a lot about

6. What does **carcasses** mean in this book?

*Before 2006, scientists could only study **carcasses**. Bodies of giant squid sometimes wash up on shore.*

A. dead bodies
B. dark images
C. living examples

Answers can be found on page 32.

GLOSSARY

beak
The mouth of a squid. It is found at the base of the mantle.

cephalopods
Ocean animals such as squid, octopuses, and cuttlefish that have soft bodies and move by squirting out water.

polar
Relating to the north or south poles.

predator
An animal that hunts and eats other animals.

prey
An animal that is hunted and eaten by another animal.

tentacles
The flexible limbs of animals such as squid.

tropical
Having weather that is often warm and wet.

FOR MORE INFORMATION

BOOKS

Pallotta, Jerry. *Whale vs. Giant Squid.* Minneapolis, MN: Abdo Publishing, 2024.

Wood, Alix. *Welcome to the Ocean.* Minneapolis, MN: Ruby Tuesday Books, 2024.

WEBSITES

Britannica Kids: Squid
kids.britannica.com/kids/article/squid/353804
Learn about all types of squid at this site.

National Geographic Kids: Giant Squid
kids.nationalgeographic.com/animals/invertebrates/facts/giant-squid
Learn more giant squid facts at this website.

Publisher's note to educators and parents: Our editors have carefully reviewed these websites to ensure that they are suitable for students. Many websites change frequently, however, and we cannot guarantee that a site's future contents will continue to meet our high standards of quality and educational value. Be advised that students should be closely supervised whenever they access the internet.

INDEX

B
beaks, 21
brains, 21

C
carcasses, 15

E
eyes, 26, 27

F
fish, 21, 23
fishing nets, 15

H
hearts, 19

I
ink, 27

K
kraken, 13

M
mantles, 17–18

O
oceans, 5, 11, 13

S
scientists, 12, 15
shrimp, 23
sperm whales, 24, 27
suction cups, 17

T
tentacles, 7, 9, 13, 17, 23

Answer Key:
1. Answers will vary; 2. Answers will vary; 3. C; 4. B; 5. C; 6. A